Art and Culture of

Ancient Rome

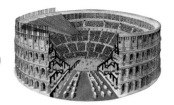

Art and Culture of

Ancient Rome

Nicholas Pistone, Giovanni Di Pasquale, and Matilde Bardi

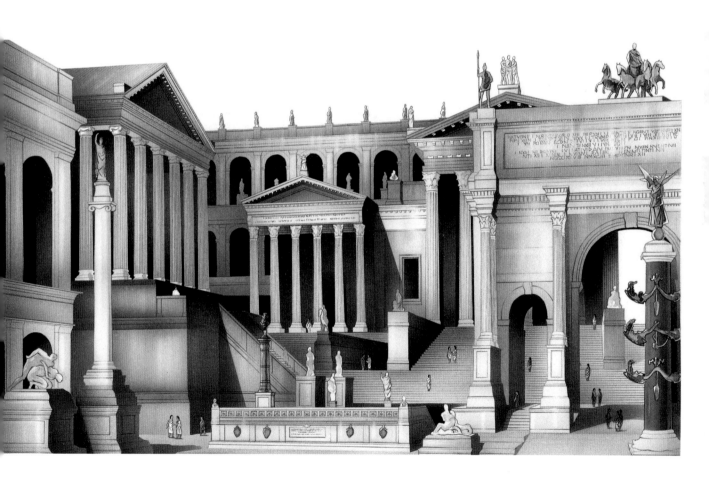

rosen publishing's
rosen
central

New York

This edition published in 2010 by:

The Rosen Publishing Group, Inc.
29 East 21st Street
New York, NY 10010

Additional end matter copyright © 2010 by The Rosen Publishing Group, Inc.

Library of Congress Cataloging-in-Publication Data

Pistone, Nicholas.
Art and culture of ancient Rome / Nicholas Pistone, Giovanni Di Pasquale, and Matilde Bardi.
    p. cm.—(Ancient art and cultures)
Includes bibliographical references and index.
ISBN 978-1-4358-3591-7 (library binding)
ISBN 978-1-61532-885-7 (pbk)
ISBN 978-1-61532-886-4 (6 pack)
1. Rome—History—Juvenile literature. 2. Rome—Social life and customs—Juvenile literature. 3. Rome—Civilization—Juvenile literature. 4. Civilization, Ancient—Juvenile literature. I. Di Pasquale, Giovanni. II. Bardi, Matilde. III. Title.
DG77.P57 2010
937—dc22

2009033053

Manufactured in the United States of America

CPSIA Compliance Information: Batch #LW10YA: For Further Information contact Rosen Publishing, New York, New York at 1-800-237-9932

Copyright © McRae Books, Florence, Italy.

Contents

Introduction 6

From the Origins to the Republic 8

The Roman Empire 10

Religion 12

Shops and Trade 14

Transport and Communication 16

War 18

Food 20

Entertainment 22

Body Care and Clothing 24

Science, Technology, and Literature 26

Art and Architecture 28

Housing 32

Roman Cities 34

Glossary 36

For More Information 37

For Further Reading 38

Index 39

Introduction

When the Romans were at the height of their power in the 2nd century CE, they governed a vast Empire that extended eastward to Mesopotamia (present-day Iraq), north and west to Britain and the Spanish peninsula, and south to the Mediterranean coast of North Africa. This immense territory was inhabited by about 50 million people. The frontiers of the Empire were well protected by a large army. All the conquered peoples – a diverse mix of different races and cultures – were subject to Roman law. Connections between Rome and the outlying areas of the Empire were maintained by a vast network of roads. At the end of the 1st century CE, Rome itself had more than one million inhabitants and was a thriving city.

The goddess Roma was a symbol of the Empire's strength. Worship of her was introduced by Emperor Augustus and was imposed on all conquered peoples. Augustus himself was declared a god after his death.

The Roman State

At the beginning of its history, Rome was a monarchy ruled successively by seven kings. In 509 BCE the monarchy was replaced by a new form of government: a republic. In a republic, all the officials are elected by the citizens. Two officials, called consuls, were chosen to be in charge of the government and the army. They discussed important political issues with an assembly called the senate. The senate was made up of wealthy landowners called patricians.

Members of the Roman senate wore a garment called a toga.

Slaves, many of whom were prisoners of war, made up over a third of the Roman population. This boy is a domestic slave.

Early conquests

By the mid-4th century BCE, the Latin people of Rome had gained control of the neighboring towns and peoples. They then turned their attention to central-southern Italy, fighting a succession of wars against the Greek and Italic peoples living there. Having conquered all of Italy, the Romans began a long war with the Carthaginians of North Africa for control of the Mediterranean, which they gained in 146 BCE.

Map showing where the ancient peoples of Italy lived.

Veneti
Ligurians
Etruscans
Italic peoples
(Latins, Umbrians, Picentini, Samnites, and others)
Rome •
Carthaginians
Apulians
Sardinians
Bruttii
Greeks
Siculians

Craftsmen produced beautiful jewelry. This cameo is the largest single piece of jewelry to survive from ancient times. It is thought to portray Emperor Tiberius and members of his family.

The Emperor

A period of civil wars, led by some army generals, brought an end to the Roman Republic. General Octavian emerged as the most powerful and introduced an imperial system of government. From 27 BCE to 14 CE, he reigned as the first Roman emperor, taking the name Augustus. The emperor held all political, religious, and administrative powers. He was backed by a huge army, and he was protected by a bodyguard of crack troops. The Empire was divided into provinces run by governors.

Victory was personified as a young girl with angel's wings. She frequently appears in Roman art, symbolizing the glory of the Empire.

Rome

Rome's greatest period of expansion took place between the 3rd and 1st centuries BCE, when the rural population poured into the city. Public buildings for conducting politics sprang up around the Forum. Emperors made it greater with temples, basilicas, arches, colonnades, libraries, and market areas. This reconstruction of the Forum in Imperial times shows the Basilica Iulia, built by Caesar (1), the Temple of Saturn, which contained the state treasury (2), the Temple of Vespasian (3), and the Temple of Concord (4). In the background is the imposing *Tabularium*, home to the state archives (5). To the right stands the Arch of Septimius Severus (6). In the foreground is the *rostra* (7), a platform used by political speakers. Numerous statues of famous people decorate the buildings.

Roman painting was heavily influenced by the Greeks. This fresco from Pompeii is a realistic portrait of a newlywed couple. Married women were responsible for running the household.

"The Pugilist" was sculpted by Apollonius of Athens, who worked in Rome during the 1st century BCE. Statues of athletes ornamented gymnasiums, Roman baths, and the villas of the rich and cultured.

The influence of the Greek world

The Romans much admired Greek culture, which had reached its zenith 400 years before the first emperor governed Rome. Many aspects of Roman daily life were copied from the Greeks, particularly their worship of gods, passion for sports, and artistic style. After the military campaigns against the Greek colonies in southern Italy, highly cultured Greek artists, writers, and poets were taken to Rome as slaves, together with Greek statues and other works of art.

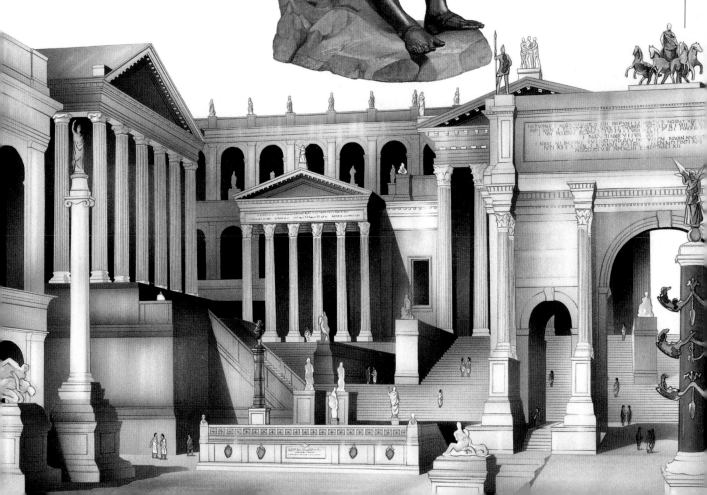

From the Origins to the Republic

According to legend, Rome was founded in 753 BCE by Romulus, who marked out a square on the Palatine Hill, on the left bank of the Tiber River. In fact, Rome was not created at a precise moment, but formed gradually as the hilltop villages near the river grew and merged. The site lay at the crossroads of two vital paths of communication. One was the salt road, which ran inland from Italy's west coast, following the course of the river. The other was the road running north-south, linking Etruria and Campania. During the 7th and 6th centuries BCE, the Romans had to fight the neighboring peoples for survival. The Etruscans, from north of Rome, took control, and the town was ruled by a succession of kings. But in 509 BCE, the Romans expelled the last king and Rome became a republic, ruled by the leading citizens. The Republic lasted for 500 years. It was marked by violent social struggles between the patricians (the ancient hereditary aristocracy) and the plebeians (everyone else). It also expanded gradually, until it controlled the whole Mediterranean basin.

The Etruscans

The Etruscans lived in the region to the north of Rome, but they extended their rule to encompass the land to the southwest, where they came into contact with Greek colonists. Both fought for control of the Mediterranean area. The Etruscans did not create a real state, but formed a league of cities. They had a highly advanced culture, and it was from them that the Romans learned, among other things, the alphabet, artistic skills, and religious practices.

This statue, probably the work of an Etruscan sculptor, portrays a leading magistrate waving to the crowd or claiming its attention.

The first inhabitants

The earliest Romans lived in a cluster of huts on the Palatine Hill above the Tiber River, and shared a communal lifestyle. Archaeologists have found objects in Rome's subsoil dating from the 8th century BCE.

An Etruscan warrior.

Rome's sixth king, Servius Tullius, is believed to have been responsible for great building activity in the city. The city was divided into four parts and surrounded by walls. Sections of the ancient walls of Rome, which in fact date from the 4th century BCE, are still described as Servian today.

The Republic

The change from monarchy to republic was marked by a detailed organization of political life. The two most senior officials were the consuls, who were in charge of the government and the army. They held office for only one year, to prevent them from becoming too ambitious. The stability of Roman politics lay in the hands of the Senate, a parliament made up of influential men from patrician families.

Map of the Roman Republic's dominions. Long and bloody wars of conquest, interrupted by a few defeats, gave the Romans control of the Mediterranean area by the end of the 2nd century BCE.

The Nile Mosaic

This mosaic from the Fortuna Sanctuary in Palestrina is one of the most important in the Greek style. The top half shows a landscape inhabited by hunters (1) and exotic and imaginary animals. Below runs the Nile River, alive with hippopotamuses (2) and crocodiles (3). The soldiers (4) in the large building with columns, between the boats and houses, are perhaps attending a visiting Roman general.

Conquests

Having conquered a large part of central Italy, Rome clashed with the most important Greek colonies in the south of the peninsula. In 281 BCE, it declared war on Taranto. Pyrrhus, king of Epirus (roughly where Albania is today), landed in Italy to support the people of Taranto. He brought a large army of soldiers, some on foot and others mounted on elephants.

A small statue of a war elephant, from Pompeii.

Julius Caesar

Julius Caesar was one of Rome's most able generals and political leaders. After conquering Gaul (now France), he led a first expedition to Britain, although this gave him little political advantage. He fought bitterly for power against his great adversary Pompey, and in 44 BCE was murdered by his political enemies in the Senate. Caesar's murder led to a series of bloody civil wars, which came to an end only when Octavian Augustus came to power as the first emperor.

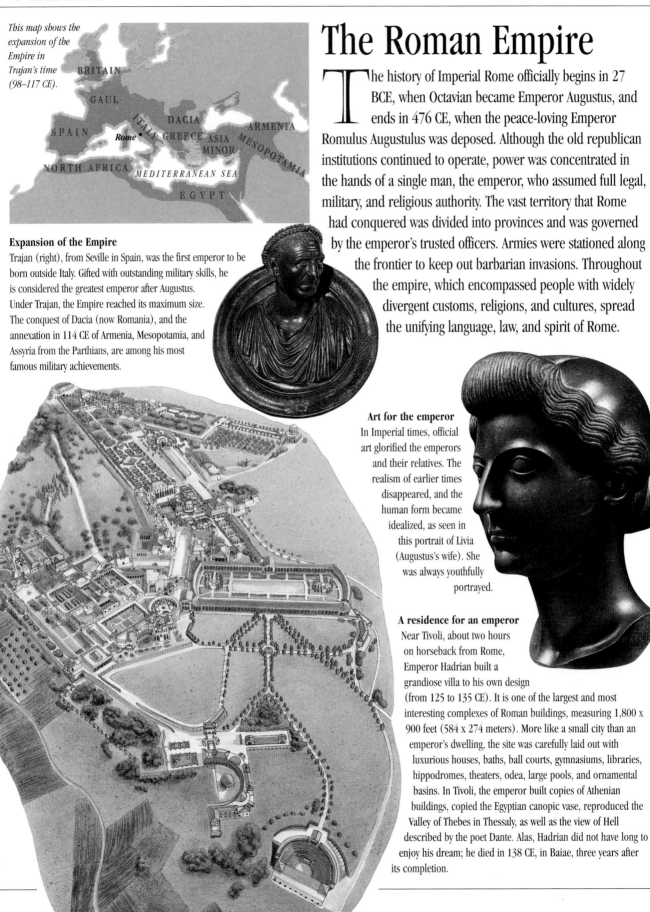

This map shows the expansion of the Empire in Trajan's time (98–117 CE).

The Roman Empire

The history of Imperial Rome officially begins in 27 BCE, when Octavian became Emperor Augustus, and ends in 476 CE, when the peace-loving Emperor Romulus Augustulus was deposed. Although the old republican institutions continued to operate, power was concentrated in the hands of a single man, the emperor, who assumed full legal, military, and religious authority. The vast territory that Rome had conquered was divided into provinces and was governed by the emperor's trusted officers. Armies were stationed along the frontier to keep out barbarian invasions. Throughout the empire, which encompassed people with widely divergent customs, religions, and cultures, spread the unifying language, law, and spirit of Rome.

Expansion of the Empire

Trajan (right), from Seville in Spain, was the first emperor to be born outside Italy. Gifted with outstanding military skills, he is considered the greatest emperor after Augustus. Under Trajan, the Empire reached its maximum size. The conquest of Dacia (now Romania), and the annexation in 114 CE of Armenia, Mesopotamia, and Assyria from the Parthians, are among his most famous military achievements.

Art for the emperor

In Imperial times, official art glorified the emperors and their relatives. The realism of earlier times disappeared, and the human form became idealized, as seen in this portrait of Livia (Augustus's wife). She was always youthfully portrayed.

A residence for an emperor

Near Tivoli, about two hours on horseback from Rome, Emperor Hadrian built a grandiose villa to his own design (from 125 to 135 CE). It is one of the largest and most interesting complexes of Roman buildings, measuring 1,800 x 900 feet (584 x 274 meters). More like a small city than an emperor's dwelling, the site was carefully laid out with luxurious houses, baths, ball courts, gymnasiums, libraries, hippodromes, theaters, odea, large pools, and ornamental basins. In Tivoli, the emperor built copies of Athenian buildings, copied the Egyptian canopic vase, reproduced the Valley of Thebes in Thessaly, as well as the view of Hell described by the poet Dante. Alas, Hadrian did not have long to enjoy his dream; he died in 138 CE, in Baiae, three years after its completion.

The Empire divided

By the 2nd century CE, the Empire had become too vast to be manageable. Increasingly frequent barbarian attacks made it steadily weaker and more vulnerable. In search of a solution, Diocletian (284–305 CE) divided the Empire into two parts, East and West. Each was governed by two men, the supreme leader, known as Augustus, and a second-in-command, called Caesar. He instituted the tetrarchy, a government composed of four men. In 330, Constantine reunited the Empire, but moved its capital to Constantinople. In 395, it was again divided and became the Western Roman Empire, with its capital in Ravenna, and the Eastern Roman Empire, with Constantinople as its capital. This division encouraged invasions by the Barbarians, and in 476 they brought about the end of the Western Roman Empire. The Eastern Empire survived for another thousand years, until 1453.

Statues of the tetrarchs: Diocletian, Maximian, Galerius, and Constantius Chlorus.

This marble inscription, a gift from the Senate and the people of Rome to Emperor Augustus, praises his virtues of courage, clemency, justice, and compassion.

SENATVS
POPVLVSQVEROMANVS
IMPCAESARIDIVIFAVGVSTO
COSVIII DEDIT CLVPEVM
VIRTVTIS CLEMENTIAE
IVSTITIAEPIETATIS ERGA
DEOSPATRIAMOVE

The Prima Porta statue of Augustus

The statue depicts Augustus raising one hand to call for silence, while in the other he holds a lance. He is wearing a decorated cuirass, or breastplate, over a military tunic. A cloak encircles his hips. The reliefs on the breastplate illustrate symbols much used by Augustus. At the top: depiction of the heavens (1); the chariot of the sun (2); Aurora and Heosphorus (3). In the central scene: a Roman general, the future emperor Tiberius, accompanied by his dog. He is greeting the king of the Parthians, Phraates IV, who is returning the military insignia taken from the Roman commander Crassus after his defeat at Carrhae in 53 BCE (4). Personification of a province, Pannonia, now Hungary, conquered and pacified by Tiberius (5); personification of Germany (6); and personification of the Earth, reclining and accompanied by two cherubs (7).

The emperor's virtues

The virtues that the people looked for in their emperor were justice, clemency, compassion, and piety (respect for the gods). Soldiers wanted to see courage and qualities of leadership. Not all the emperors were equal to the task. Nero, Caligula, and Domitian (1st century CE) were guilty of many crimes of injustice. But Titus (1st century CE) earned himself the title "delight of mankind"; Antoninus was called Antoninus Pius; and Marcus Aurelius (2nd century CE), who fought ceaselessly to defend the Empire's integrity, was considered a wise and gentle man.

This cameo shows a Roman soldier fighting the Barbarians.

Religion

The early Romans worshiped the gods who presided over farming and social activities. Through contact with the Etruscan civilization, they gradually adopted new gods, especially Jove, Juno, and Minerva. After conquering the Greek colonies in the South of Italy, the Romans also absorbed some of the Greek gods. The official religion of the Romans was formal, rather than spiritual, and did not offer comfort in this life or the next. Perhaps because of this, during the time of the Empire, various gods from Egypt and Asia began to be worshiped. The Egyptian goddess Isis and the Syrian cult of Mithra (the sun god) became popular. An Asian goddess named Cybele, the mother of the gods, was also worshiped. Then, in 391 CE, Christianity was declared the official religion of the Empire.

The Greek gods

Through contact with the Greeks, the Romans came to worship the Olympian gods of Greece. Zeus, for example, became identified with the Roman god Jove, and Hera with Juno. Others included Apollo, Demeter (Ceres to the Romans), Dionysus (Bacchus), Aphrodite (Venus), and Hermes (Mercury). Even Greek heroes like Heracles became a Roman god (Hercules).

Statue of Isis, 2nd century CE. In one hand she holds a sistrum (a musical instrument), and in the other a small vase containing the life-giving waters of the Nile River.

The Roman god Jove became associated with the Greek god Zeus. He was considered to be above all other gods.

Egyptian gods

During the 1st century CE, worship of the Egyptian goddess Isis and her husband, Osiris, began to spread all over the Roman world. According to myth, Isis brought Osiris back to life, and this gave people hope of a life after death.

The cult of Cybele, the "Great Mother" of the gods, came to Rome in 205 BCE and was popular in Imperial times.

The sanctuary

The sanctuary of Palestrina, built in the late 2nd century BCE, was the largest religious complex to be built during the Republican era. It was built on six artificial terraces cut into the slope of a hill. Staircases and colonnaded corridors led up to the sixth terrace, where a double colonnade surrounded a large open square. At one end of this was a theater space, and on the summit stood a round temple containing a statue of the goddess Fortuna Primigenia, to whom the site was dedicated.

A circular temple to Vesta, the goddess of the domestic hearth. She protected the all-important household fire.

Bronze statuettes of two Lares, who traditionally guarded the boundaries of a home.

Festivals

Ceremonies were performed to ensure the goodwill of the gods, which was believed to be vital to the well-being of the state. Days reserved for ceremonies were recorded on a calendar (above). Capital letters marked the days thought to be favorable for public religious festivals, and unlucky days were also marked. October 19th was chosen for the ceremonial cleansing of weapons, and March 23rd for trumpets – festivals held to gain the favor of the gods before a battle. If a mistake was made during the performance of the rituals, they had to be repeated from the beginning.

In the many surviving examples of Roman Christian art, Jesus Christ is often portrayed as the Good Shepherd.

Christianity

Between the 1st and 2nd centuries CE, Christianity reached Rome. It found favor among the poorer people, who began to gather together to perform the new rites. Christians were persecuted for a long time because they refused to recognize the divinity of the emperor. The first official persecutions took place under the rule of Emperor Nero, who blamed the Christians for the serious fire that destroyed much of Rome in 64 CE. They continued until 313 CE, when Emperor Constantine proclaimed Christianity the official religion of the Empire.

Private worship

Family worship was less formal and more deeply felt than the official religion. Every Roman house had a small altar dedicated to the *Manes*, or souls of ancestors; the *Penates*, spirits who protected the household goods; and the *Lares*, who watched over the fields and roads around a home. The household hearth was dedicated to Vesta. Rituals were performed to keep the favor of these gods.

The altar of Domitianus Aenobarbus

This frieze from the 1st century BCE decorated the sides of a monument, possibly an altar. It is adorned with figures from the wedding of Neptune, the sea god, and is the only example of historic sculpture left from Republican times. In this scene, the ritual sacrifice of animals is being conducted to please Mars, the god of war, at the start of a military campaign. The animals were sacrificed in exchange for divine protection, in a ritual that remained unchanged for centuries. On the left of a sacrificial altar (1) is Mars (2) and two musicians (3). On the right is a magistrate (4), assisted by *Camilli*, the carriers of sacred objects (5). The magistrate is about to sacrifice an ox, a sheep, and a pig, which are led by *Vittimari*, the sacrificial slaughterers (6).

Mercury was the god of trade and merchants, and also (perhaps not by chance) the god of thieves and swindlers. He was portrayed wearing a winged hat, and carrying a staff entwined with two serpents and a bag.

Stores and storekeepers

Most stores were run by families of slaves on behalf of their owners, or by freedmen, who were slaves that had been released. The storekeepers often lived above their shops. Most stores sold food – there were bakers, butchers, grocery stores, rotisseries, and so on. But many shops also acted as studios and workshops for goldsmiths, perfume makers, shoemakers, weavers, marble-workers, and carpenters.

This funerary frieze shows a woman preparing poultry, pigs, and a rabbit for sale.

Shops and Trade

People in the Roman world practiced many different trades. We know about them both from literature and from the carved stone reliefs that decorated funeral monuments. In the ruined cities of Pompeii and Herculaneum – both buried by the eruption of Vesuvius in 79 CE – actual shops were preserved, as well as the reliefs and frescoes that advertised each kind of business. Some of these show people at work in their shops, suggesting that production was mostly small-scale. A rare example of a state industry was the making of military equipment.

Fresco of a bakery, from Pompeii.

Goods were weighed on scales before being sold. The scales were made from a metal bar with a sliding weight at one end and a plate for the goods at the other end. Strict controls aimed to prevent sellers from cheating their customers by using false weights. The unit for measuring weight was the pound.

City markets

The Forum in Rome was the center of trade in the city, as well as a meeting place and political arena. All businesses were represented there, especially money exchanges. Between 113 and 117 CE, Emperor Trajan built Rome's last and most impressive Forum. It housed a basilica, two libraries, and the extensive market (right) with its 150 shops on four stories – just like a modern shopping mall.

Craftworkers

Most handicraft work was carried out in small workshops by semiskilled workers. Blacksmiths were in great demand because they made tools for other craftsmen as well as everyday items such as knives, locks, and containers. Craftworkers in each trade belonged to a guild, or professional association. There were more than 150 guilds in Imperial Rome.

A knife seller displaying his goods.

A textile merchant displays his fabrics. Embroidered materials and cushions hang from the ceiling.

Stele of a blacksmith from Aquileia

This relief shows the inside of a blacksmith's workshop, together with a sample of his products. An assistant (1) is rekindling the fire in the forge (2) using bellows. He is standing behind a protective screen (3). The blacksmith is using a hammer (4) to beat the metal on the anvil (5). To the right are some tools of the trade: a hammer and tongs (6). Beneath these are two workshop products: a lance tip and a lock (7).

Coins were decorated with the heads of emperors, gods, or historical events.

A river boat transporting barrels. The boat is steered by a man at the stern; a slave on the river bank tows it forward.

Currency

About 320 BCE, the first money changers appeared in Rome's Forum, and in 269 BCE the first mint was set up to make new coins. Emperor Augustus introduced the first Imperial coins. The most valuable was the gold *aureus*, equal to 25 silver *denarii*. One *denarius* was worth 4 brass *sesterces* or 16 bronze *asses*. One *asse* would buy a loaf of bread. The annual salary of a legionary soldier was 900 *sesterces*.

Trading routes

Goods for trade were mostly transported by boat along coastlines or rivers – a far cheaper, quicker, and safer method than road transport. Foodstuffs from all over the Empire arrived at the port of Ostia, near Rome. Grain from Egypt was particularly important, and was brought by a convoy of cargo ships. Sailing boats and barges carried the goods up the Tiber River to Rome.

Transport and Communication

A vast network of roads connected the countries under Roman rule. The Romans built their roads in straight lines for long distances, however harsh the landscape. Some sections were steeply sloping, and bridges and tunnels were built where necessary to overcome obstacles along the way. The straight routes were not connected by curves, but instead intersected at angles. Soldiers were able to move relatively quickly along the road network to any trouble spots in the vast Empire, helping to ensure its safety. In fact, not just armies, but raw materials, goods, news carriers, private citizens, and ideas marched along the Roman roads.

Road building

Road builders (often soldiers) started by marking out two parallel tracks about 10 to 14 feet (3–4.2 m) apart. Then they dug down between the tracks until they reached a solid foundation. The trench was generally filled in with four layers of material, which gave good drainage: sand and lime (1); clay and stones (2); pebbles with terracotta fragments (3); and finally wide flint or lava stones (4), which were carefully positioned to make as smooth a surface as possible. If the foundation was marshy, support poles were set into the ground and extra layers of pebbles, sand, mortar, and bundles of sticks were used (5).

This map shows the main routes linking Rome with the most distant parts of the Empire. Many modern roads follow the same routes.

Every 1,000 paces along a main road stood a cylindrical milestone, which marked the distance to the next town.

The Appian Way

Perhaps the most famous of all Roman roads is the Appian Way. Ordered by the consul Appius Claudius Caecus (hence "Appian"), and opened in 312 BCE, it originally ran southeast from Rome for about 125 miles (200 kilometers). During the reign of Emperor Trajan, it was extended nearly 200 miles (322 km) to Brindisi, a major port on the southeast tip of Italy and an important link to Greece. A paved section of the original Appian Way, about 14 feet (4.2 m) wide, still survives near Rome.

Detail from the Peutinger Map, a medieval copy of a Roman map from the 4th to 5th centuries CE. The southern tip of Italy is in the center, with Sicily below it and North Africa at the bottom. Roads are shown as straight lines.

Bridges

The Romans used their expertise at building arches to build many impressive bridges and aqueducts. The Milvian Bridge crosses the Tiber River in Rome, and it is the start of the Via Flaminia – a road that ran north across Italy to the Adriatic coast.

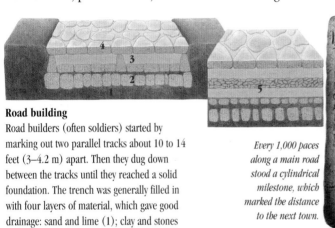

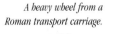

A heavy wheel from a Roman transport carriage.

Relief of a port, about 200 CE. Goods are being unloaded from a ship with lowered sails (on the right). Another ship is coming into port, while its crew performs sacrifices of thanksgiving. In the center stands Neptune, god of the sea, holding his trident.

Methods of transport

Many people traveled on foot along the Roman roads, carrying luggage by hand or on the backs of mules or horses. For long distances, they rode in carriages pulled by two horses or donkeys. There was room to sit or lie down in a carriage. Nobles sent messengers ahead of them to organize the changeover of horses, or to arrange stopovers either at friends' houses or at one of the numerous hotels and inns.

Ports

Goods were brought to Italy by sea from all over the Empire and beyond. They mainly arrived at the ports of Pozzuoli (near Naples) and Ostia – the most important port – just outside Rome, at the mouth of the Tiber River. Cargo ships arrived from Egypt laden with grain, whale oil, wine, and luxury goods from North Africa and Spain. With a good wind, a ship could sail from Carthage to Ostia in 3 to 5 days. Ships from Alexandria took 15 to 20 days. Gades (Cadiz) in Spain provided a market for products from countries on the Atlantic coast.

Painting of a river boat used between Rome and the nearby port of Ostia.

View of a port

This 1st century fresco from Stabia, south of Rome, shows a thriving Italian port. Some men are fishing on the rocks (1) near the lighthouse (2). At the entrance to the port is a pier supported by arches (3). Some boats are moored in the port with their sails lowered (4). In the distance is another pier (5), and within the majestic city stands a row of statues on top of columns (6). This type of landscape painting was very popular; scenes often included views of promontories, rivers, temples, mountains, and pastoral activities.

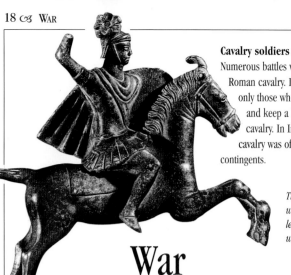

Cavalry soldiers
Numerous battles were won thanks to the Roman cavalry. In the Republican era, only those who could afford to buy and keep a horse joined the cavalry. In Imperial times, the cavalry was often made up of allied contingents.

The sword was the basic weapon of the Roman legionary. Short and thick, it was called a gladius.

The legions
A legion was divided into separate units. There were three ranks of infantry, grouped according to strength and age. First came the lance-bearers (*maniples*), followed by the *princeps*, who were young and strong, and behind them came the older, more experienced soldiers (*triarii*). All legionaries were armed with a javelin, sword, shield, and breastplate. The emblem of the legion was the eagle, a symbol of Jupiter.

War

Discipline, organization, and technology formed the basis of Roman military victories. The basic army unit was the legion (originally 4,200, and later 6,000 infantry). The legion was divided into 10 cohorts (with about 500 men in each). A cohort was subdivided into three *maniples*, each made up of two centuries (a century was 100 men). On the flanks of each legion rode the cavalry and allied contingents. Six officers, called military tribunes, were appointed by the consul (the top army official) to recruit the right number of men for the legion. In the first few centuries of its history, Rome did not have a permanent army. But by the beginning of the 1st century BCE, Roman armies had transformed themselves into professional military units trained for all types of battle. The Roman army was as efficient as any well-trained modern army.

Forts
Roman forts were always laid out in the same way, whether they were permanent walled structures or temporary camps. The camp was square, and was crossed from north-to-south and east-to-west by two main roads. Gates guarded the entrances to the camp. The camp was surrounded by a ditch. Stones and earth dug from the ditch were piled up to form a bank, or rampart. Along the top of the rampart, wooden stakes were hammered into the ground to make a strong fence. Sentries kept watch along the rampart by day and night.

Reconstruction of one of the forts along Hadrian's Wall in northern Britain. Inside were soldiers' barracks, commanders' quarters, baths, and a temple.

This tablet commemorates the building of a fortress by the 20th legion, stationed near Hadrian's Wall. It shows Mars and Hercules, the gods associated with war.

Hadrian's Wall
Hadrian's Wall marked the northern boundary of the Roman Empire. It ran east-west for 73 miles (112 km) across Northern Britain. The wall measured 7 to 10 feet (2.1–3 m) thick and 16 to 20 feet (4.9–6.1 m) high. A trench on the southern side and a moat on the northern side were dug 39 feet (11.8 m) wide and up to 13 feet (5.8 m) deep. At irregular intervals along the wall, towers, sentry posts, forts, and military encampments were built for the 11,500 soldiers. Much of the wall is still standing.

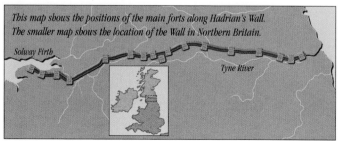

This map shows the positions of the main forts along Hadrian's Wall. The smaller map shows the location of the Wall in Northern Britain.

Solway Firth

Tyne River

Detail from Trajan's Column

Emperor Trajan's conquest of Dacia (north of the Danube River in part of present-day Romania) is described in great detail on Trajan's Column (see p. 28). On the lower left, Trajan, lance in hand, celebrates the victorious outcome of a battle with his soldiers (1); next to him is the emblem of the legion, the eagle (2). To his right are two Germans (3) and a group of Dacians on horseback (4). Trajan (5) is also shown talking to Dacian ambassadors (6) in front of a Roman camp. In the upper section, two large Roman boats (7) are rowed by oarsmen up the Danube. The emperor (8) is steering one of them. After landing next to a fortified town (9), the soldiers unload weapons and supplies (10). Some have already started to march (11).

The triumphs

Victorious generals paraded in the Forum with their troops, showing off prisoners of war and seized goods. In this relief – part of the decoration from the Titus Arch in Rome – a procession of soldiers carries treasures seized from the Temple of Jerusalem in 70 CE. In the foreground is a seven-branched candelabra from the temple.

Naval battles

Battleships were armed with an underwater triple-pronged bronze ram (*rostrum*). This was used to ram the keels of enemy ships. Gangways (*corvii*) about 26 feet (7.6 m) long were attached to the ship's stern so that soldiers could cross over to the enemy ship and fight in hand-to-hand combat.

This column commemorates the Romans' great naval victory over the Carthaginians at Milazzo in 260 BCE. It is mounted with the rams of the defeated ships.

War machines

The Romans adopted the attack weapons used by the Greeks. Mobile towers mounted with battering rams were used for knocking down enemy walls, ballistas for hurling heavy rocks, and catapults for showering the enemy with darts, arrows, burning missiles, and stones.

Wine

The Romans learned from the Greek colonists in Southern Italy how to cultivate vines (right). They developed the skill until they had about 30 different kinds of wine. It was usually watered down and served warm. The wine was heated in bronze containers or terracotta pots like this one (left).

Food

In early Roman times, people mostly ate cereals, vegetables dressed with olive oil, small amounts of meat, and large quantities of fruit – a diet that today is described as "Mediterranean." But in the days of Imperial Rome, cooking became an art form, and tracts were written on the subject. New ingredients were imported from abroad, such as precious spices from the East. An aromatic herb named *silphium* was brought at great expense from Cyrene, a city in North Africa. And *garum*, a sauce made from sun-dried fish, was also highly prized. Lavish banquets were eaten by the rich. Starters might include egg dishes, seafood, and snails. These were followed by a first main course (*mensa*) of roast or stewed meat, saltwater or freshwater fish, and birds such as stuffed peacocks or swans. At the end of the meal, after the fruit and sweetmeats (the second *mensa*), a blend of wine and honey (*mulsum*) was served.

Fruit

Fruit was always served at the end of a Roman meal in elegant baskets or glass bowls. Italy produced an abundance of apples, pears, cherries, plums, figs, walnuts, almonds, pomegranates, and chestnuts. Dates and apricots were imported from Africa and Asia Minor.

Agriculture

Agriculture was the backbone of the economy in the Roman world, and it was considered a noble activity. For many centuries the main crops were spelt (a low-quality, single-grain wheat), millet, wheat, barley, vines, and olives. Fruit trees were also grown. Writers such as Cato, Varro, and Columella left written accounts of farming practices that remained unchanged for centuries until the arrival of modern technology.

Mosaic showing farmers at work plowing, sowing, and tending vines.

A centuries-old loaf found in Pompeii. Made from white flour, it was the "luxury" bread.

Eggs

The Romans kept hens for their eggs. They also ate the eggs of geese, ducks, and wild birds. Special pans like this one were used for cooking them.

Bread

The Romans had about 20 different kinds of bread. The most expensive was white bread made from fine flour. Ordinary people ate a dark bread made with bran, which even the poorest could afford. The first bakeries appeared in 171 BCE. Before that, bread was baked at home by the women of the household.

In this bas-relief of a butcher's shop, a woman keeps charge of the money, while a man cuts chops with a cleaver. Next to him are scales for weighing the meat.

This 1st century CE fresco from Pompeii shows a table set with precious silverware.

Kinds of meat

Pork was preferred to all other kinds of meat, and every part of the pig was eaten. Other popular choices were lamb, goat, goose, chicken, rabbit, and pigeon. Beef remained strictly banned for centuries because oxen were needed to work the fields. Their slaughter was considered a crime. The favorite wild game were boar and deer, and birds such as thrush, partridge, and quail.

On this portable stove, meat could be cooked on the bars, like a barbecue.

Pots, plates, and cups

Cooking implements were simple, and were hung on the wall above the water basin or the firebrick cooking surface. There were cauldrons and various types of bronze pots; terracotta pots called *amphorae* for storing wine, water, or oil; terracotta dishes and jugs with lids; and glass containers for honey (the only sweetener) and salt. In wealthier households, the tableware included pewter or glazed ceramic plates, glass bottles and drinking glasses, and colored glass jugs and goblets.

Silver and bronze pans from two sets of tableware. They came from Pompeii and date from the 1st century CE.

Mosaic of fish

Fish came into the Roman diet fairly late, but by the 2nd century BCE large quantities of mollusks (e.g. oysters and clams), crustaceans (e.g. crabs, lobsters, and shrimp), and other fish were eaten. Fish farms supplied the tables of the rich, at great expense. This beautiful 1st century mosaic from Pompeii includes an octopus and a lobster fighting (1), a moray eel (2), a squid (3), a murex shell (4), a skate (5), a red mullet (6), a sea bass (7), and a Mediterranean gilthead (8). All of these sea creatures could be caught in the Bay of Naples.

Theater

Livius Andronicus, a Greek slave from the 3rd century BCE, is traditionally credited with bringing Greek tragedies and comedies to Rome. Naevius and Ennius were the major writers of Roman tragedies; Plautus, later followed by Terence, wrote comedies, whose liveliness and realism guarantee them regular performances today.

Entry tickets (tesserae) to the theater.

Free and paid entry

Arenas and circuses were public entertainments, and entry was free. Theaters and *odea* needed an inexpensive ticket, which allowed the actors to support themselves.

The theater of Marcellus in Rome was begun by Julius Caesar, and is still standing. It has a semicircular area of 1,400 square feet (130 sq m), and was originally about 100 feet (36.4 m) high. It held up to 10,000 spectators.

Preparing for a satirical drama

This mosaic from Pompeii shows actors getting ready for a performance. The chorusmaster (and perhaps playwright) (1) is watching two actors in goatskin costumes practicing their dance steps (2), while a costumed musician plays the double flute (3). To the right, an actor is getting changed (4). Masks (5) from the drama are in a box on the floor next to the chorusmaster.

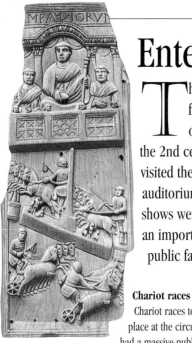

Entertainment

The Romans enjoyed a great number of feast days – 65 a year during the reign of Emperor Augustus, rising to 135 in the 2nd century. On feast days, huge crowds visited the circus, the amphitheater, theaters, or auditoriums (where music was played). The shows were not only a citizen's right, but also an important way for the government to win public favor.

The Romans loved gambling with dice. They would bet on charioteers at the circus, gladiators in the arena, and on fights between dogs or roosters. These two roosters are about to fight. The bag on the table contains the betting money.

Chariot races

Chariot races took place at the circus and had a massive public following. Two-horse (*biga*) and four-horse (*quadriga*) chariots had to complete seven circuits of the track, racing counterclockwise around the central barrier, or "spine," which had two semi-circular ends. The charioteers rode standing up, holding the reins to steer the carriage in their left hand, and the whip to spur on the horses in their right hand.

A 1st century CE sculpture of hunting dogs attacking a stag. It was found in Herculaneum.

Hunting

Hunting was introduced to Rome in 252 BCE, and was a common amphitheater entertainment. It involved fights between animals, or between animals and men. Animals were usually paired with their natural predators: deer with dogs, for example, or gazelles with lions. But sometimes the combinations were unnatural, such as tigers with bears.

Gladiators

Gladiators were generally prisoners of war or criminals. They were trained to fight, often to the death, in the arena. The various categories of gladiators were named for their weapons, or for the way they fought. The *Retiarus* carried a net and a trident, and his usual enemy, the *Pursuer*, wore a helmet and carried a shield and sickle. The *Mirmillion* had only a sword and helmet, while the *Hoplomachi* wore just heavy armor.

This fresco from a house in Pompeii shows the "pitch invasion" that took place at a gladiator contest in 59 CE, when spectators from Pompeii and Nocera started fighting each other. As a punishment, the amphitheater was closed for 10 years.

Fans

The atmosphere in a Roman circus, or amphitheater, was similar to that of a modern sports' stadium. The best gladiators were idolized, and they made large fortunes. Charioteers were contracted to particular stables, or to different parties (white, red, green, and blue), each of which had its own fanatical supporters.

Music

Music was played on many private and public occasions, such as banquets, religious ceremonies, or celebrations of military victories. Concerts were held in the *odea* (singular *odeon*), and many people lived as traveling musicians.

Mosaic showing a company of traveling musicians, from a house known as "Menandro's" in Pompeii. The musicians are playing a tambourine, a double flute, and crotals – small bronze cymbals that were clashed together to make a tinkling noise. The boy is playing some kind of wind instrument.

Body Care and Clothing

From the 1st century CE, Roman women began to wear makeup on their eyes, lips, and cheeks. They applied beauty masks to their faces and had body massages. Balsams, ointments, and perfumes were very popular. Wealthy women wore heavy jewelry – earrings, bracelets, necklaces, clasps, and hairpins – made of gold and set with pearls, semiprecious stones, or imitation gems (glass paste). Men also took great care of their bodies, and young men worked out at the gym. Everyone went to the public baths.

Painting of a young girl pouring perfume into a flask, or ampulla.

At the baths, women did exercises in the gym or relaxed in a tub. They wore costumes very similar to a modern bikini.

Young people who went to the gym used an instrument called a strigil to scrape off the oils and sweat after they had finished exercising.

Perfume

Perfume was used extensively both at home and in public places. It came down with theater curtains and was sprayed liberally at banquets. It was also used at funeral services and during sacrifices. Perfume-makers extracted scents from flowers, shrubs, plants, and roots, either by simply squeezing them or by leaving them to soak in oil or fat. Particularly in demand were perfumes from the East, which were as expensive as pearls or gems, even though they quickly dissolved and disappeared.

At the baths

The first public Roman baths (*thermae*) were modeled on those of the Greeks. Although they appeared late, they soon became not just a place to look after the body, but somewhere to meet friends and relax. City-dwellers could exercise, and then thoroughly cleanse themselves by sweating out skin impurities, which were scraped away – the Romans did not have soap.

Fresco showing weavers at work

Weaving was one of the most important Roman craft industries. This painting from Pompeii shows a group of weavers at work. One person is unraveling lengths of wool (teasing) so that they can be evenly cut (1); another is carrying on his head a wooden apparatus used to stretch the material, so that it could be steamed with sulfur to make it as white as possible (2). The owl is a symbol of the goddess Athena, protector of the wool-workers' guild (3).

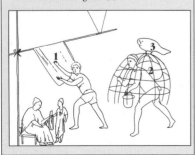

Ladies with a fan and a parasol, from a 4th century BCE vase.

Women's clothes

In early Republican times, both men and women wore togas. But before long, standard clothing for women was a tunic covered by a foot-length, pleated gown (*stola*), tied at the waist with a belt. In Imperial times, a new fashion appeared for wearing a wide, embroidered cloak (*palla*) in a bright shade of red, yellow, or blue.

In Imperial times, many women covered all or part of their hair with a cap made of fine gold netting. Hairpins were commonly used to pin up curls.

Hairstyles

Until the 1st century CE, women mostly wore their hair straight. Married women tied it back, while young unmarried girls wore it loose. Later on, a fashion for curls developed. These were gathered and pinned up high on the head. Such complicated hairstyles required the skills of a servant. Sometimes natural hairpieces were used to add volume.

Portrait of a woman from the second half of the 1st century CE, wearing an imposing hairstyle.

A gold clasp from the 4th century, made from two pieces that click together.

A mirror was a must-have for any lady's dressing table. It was made from metal so highly polished that it reflected a person's face. This long-handled silver mirror dates from the 1st century CE.

Shoes

Men and women wore either hobnailed ankle boots (below) or shoes that reached the bridge of the foot. Made from leather, they were fastened by four strings that tied around the ankle or leg. Only senators were allowed to wear black shoes, while high magistrates (consuls, praetors, and censors) could wear red shoes. Sandals were worn indoors. Soldiers' shoes had leather-stringed tops, and the soles were reinforced with nails, which made them last longer on cross-country marches.

Jewelry

Rings, pendants, necklaces, and earrings were just a few of the ornaments worn by a fashionable Roman woman. Made from precious metals and set with artificial gems, real gems, or amber, they reached such extreme proportions that in the 2nd century BCE, the censors issued a law banning jewelry that was over a certain weight.

A lady wearing fine jewelry, from a fresco in the Imperial palace of Trier.

Science, Technology, and Literature

The Romans may not have been experts at developing new technology, but they excelled in architecture – designing and building all kinds of magnificent structures, including important civic works such as aqueducts. Medicine was based on past knowledge and practice of the Greeks, and only began to be considered a scientific discipline at the end of the 1st century BCE. During the 3rd century BCE, Roman literature emerged as an art form, again in imitation of the Greeks. By the late-Republican era, poetic works, histories, and speeches were being written that were to have an enormous influence on writers of later centuries.

Votive offering to the gods for healing a leg.

In this remarkable fusion of art and science, Atlas – a figure from Greek mythology – holds up a globe of the heavens, marked with the known constellations and zones of the zodiac.

A bronze surgical instrument from Pompeii. Wounds and injuries (especially those received in war) were treated by surgeons, almost all of whom were trained in Greece.

Medicine

To protect their health, the Romans prayed to the goddess Salus and the god Aesculepius (the Greek Asclepius). Doctors used herbs, medicinal plants, and diets to heal the sick. Galen of Pergamum – the personal physician of Emperor Marcus Aurelius – is the most famous name in Roman medicine. His *Ars Medica* remained a classic textbook for doctors.

Astronomy

The Romans learned how to observe and study the heavens from the Etruscans and from Eastern peoples. Astrologers measured time, and strict links were established between the movements of the stars and events in the farming calendar.

Literature

The golden age of Latin literature was the 1st century BCE. Virgil was one of the major poets (70–19 BCE). In his epic poem *Aeneid*, he wrote about the founding of Rome. He also wrote many poems celebrating the fertility of the soil, in line with Emperor Augustus's political program for a return to work on the land. Marcus Tullius Cicero (106–43 BCE), a leading political figure, is considered one of the greatest speech-makers of the ancient world. Many of his speeches are still studied today as examples of grammatical correctness.

Bust of Cicero.

This fresco is inspired by an episode in Virgil's epic Aeneid. *It shows a doctor using an instrument to extract an arrowhead from Aeneas's leg.*

A mosaic of Virgil, seated.

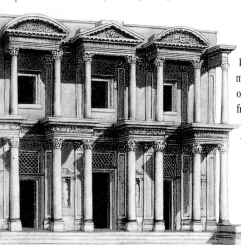

Libraries

From late-Republican times, libraries multiplied in Rome and other major cities of the Empire. Founded by donations from private citizens, they contained texts for literary or technical instruction, written in Latin and Greek.

The library at Ephesus was built early in the 1st century CE by the heirs of a city magistrate, who left a sum of money for the purchase of volumes.

Studies

The study of literature formed the basis of the education of young Romans. A knowledge of grammar and oratory (public speaking) was essential for a political or administrative career.

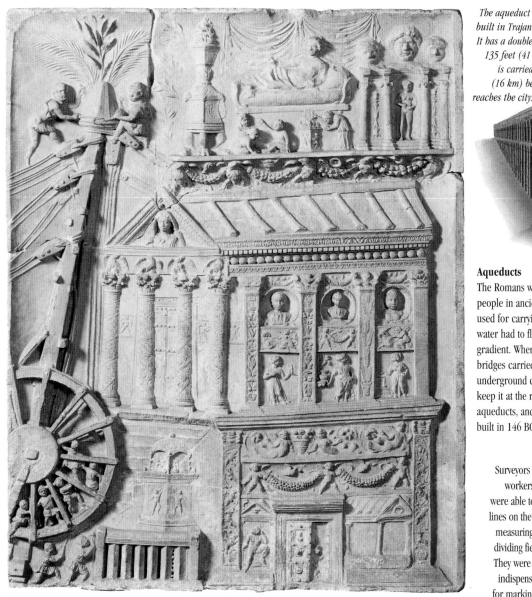

The aqueduct in Segovia (2nd century CE) was built in Trajan's time, and is still in use today. It has a double row of arches measuring 135 feet (41 m) high. The water is carried for 10 miles (16 km) before it reaches the city.

Aqueducts

The Romans were the first people in ancient times to build aqueducts, used for carrying fresh water to towns. The water had to flow along a continuously gentle gradient. Where necessary, high-arched bridges carried it across dips in the land, and underground channels took it through rock to keep it at the right level. Rome had 11 aqueducts, and one of these, the Aqua Marcia, built in 146 BCE, still operates today.

Measuring the ground

Surveyors were highly skilled and respected workers. Using a special instrument, they were able to trace straight lines on the ground for measuring and dividing fields. They were also indispensable for marking out the routes of new Roman roads.

Relief of a building site

One of the most spectacular machines for raising weights was the treadmill crane, so-called because it was operated by the pressure of feet turning a great wheel (1). Slaves (2) produced energy by "walking" around inside the wheel. This worked a winch (3), which was able to lift amazingly heavy loads using a system of pulleys (4) and ropes (5). The branch of a tree (6) has been hoisted to the top of the crane to celebrate the completion of the building (7).

Mills

The mill at Barbegal in France dates back to the 4th century CE. A series of waterwheels, each more than 7 feet (2.1 m) in diameter, were connected by a simple system of gears to horizontal grinding stones. These ground enough flour for the town's 80,000 inhabitants.

This mosaic from Hadrian's villa at Tivoli, outside Rome, depicts doves drinking water from a golden goblet – a popular theme in Roman times.

Mosaics

Many of the mosaics that have survived today are copies of famous frescoes from the Greek world. Early mosaics were made on floors using pebbles. Later, they were used to decorate walls and vaults as well, and were made with stone cubes, marble tablets, or glass paste. Admired for their elegant designs and bright colors, mosaics soon became an essential feature in any place of luxury.

This statue of Emperor Marcus Aurelius is one of the most famous statues of Roman times.

Painting

Many examples of Roman paintings have survived, especially from the 1st century BCE. Some of the best preserved are the frescoes in Livius's House in Rome, and frescoes in the houses of Pompeii and Herculaneum. Rooms in Roman houses were decorated with frescoes of all different sizes. They ranged from simple colored panels to large, populated scenes, delicate miniatures, and fantastical architectural designs. The biggest cycle of paintings comes from the Villa dei Misteri in Pompeii.

Art and Architecture

The Romans learned many artistic skills from Greek art and often elaborated on Greek themes in their own art. They were also influenced by the cultures of the Etruscans and Italic peoples of pre-Republican times. Much Roman art was commissioned to celebrate military conquests and to glorify public figures. Historical narrative friezes decorated columns and arches, and sculpted busts and statues were prominently displayed in public places. Artists also painted colorful scenes on the inner walls of houses. Throughout the Empire, temples, aqueducts, circuses, baths, and amphitheaters attested to the greatness of Roman architecture.

Portrait of an unknown man, from Osimo (Ancona).

Sculpture

During the 1st century BCE, Roman sculpture was heavily influenced both by the Greeks and by the Etruscan and Italic peoples of early Italy. The facial features of emperors, magistrates, soldiers, and ordinary people were faithfully reproduced in minute detail, and displayed in public places or on funerary monuments.

This 4th century sarcophagus, or coffin, made from porphyry, is sculpted with scenes showing a Roman victory against the barbarians. It may once have belonged to an emperor, but was later used as a tomb for Saint Helen, mother of Emperor Constantine.

Trajan's Column

Erected in 113 CE, Trajan's Column commemorates Emperor Trajan's victories in the Dacian wars. The twisting column is 98 feet (29.8 m) high. It was originally surmounted by a gold and bronze statue of the emperor (reached by climbing 185 steps). Trajan's tomb was in a room at the base of the column. The column itself is made of 19 blocks of marble placed one on top of the other, and decorated with a 656-foot-long (200-meter-long) narrative frieze. The detailed scenes show Trajan and his army fighting battles, marching, building military encampments, and delivering prisoners. So realistic are the pictures that it is almost like looking at a visual news report.

Sarcophagi (coffins)

The resting places of emperors and their relatives were often large, tomb-like sarcophagi, or coffins, decorated with reliefs glorifying the dead person. In the 4th and 5th centuries CE, they became common for ordinary people as well because Christianity chose to bury the dead instead of cremating the bodies. Marble or red porphyry were favored, as both types of stone sculpted well.

Garden Fresco from the House of the Golden Bracelet
Roman naturalist painters made the painting of garden scenes a respected art. Specializing in painting plants and animals, they recreated scenes from nature on the floors and walls of many Roman homes. This fresco from the 1st century CE decorated a room in Pompeii. It shows a lattice fence, and behind that a fountain (possibly a birdbath) surrounded by numerous plant and bird species. Among the birds are a swallow (1), a pigeon (2), a magpie (3), sparrows (4–5), and a blackbird (6). The shrubbery includes ivy (7), laurel (8), oleander (9), and palm (10).

Art and literature
Roman painters were inspired both by Greek myths and by Roman literature, such as Virgil's *Aeneid* and Ovid's *Metamorphoses*. This fresco (below) illustrates an episode from Hercules's childhood: the boy proves to his amazed father how strong he is by strangling a serpent.

Fresco of the boy Hercules, from the Vettii house in Pompeii.

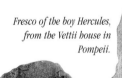

Influence of other cultures
Roman art was influenced by the Etruscans, the Greeks, and later on by Eastern cultures. This statue of Antinous, Emperor Hadrian's favorite (117–138 CE), was sculpted in the Egyptian style.

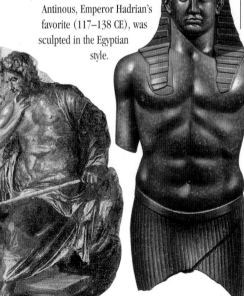

The Pantheon in Rome

The Pantheon is an extraordinary piece of architecture, built in honor of all the gods. It was commissioned by Emperor Hadrian at the start of the 2nd century CE, and was built on top of an earlier building ordered by Marcus Agrippa (Augustus's general and son-in-law). It incorporates a mix of architectural styles, including a Greek portico over the main entrance (1). The inside is circular, and the floor has a diameter of 142 feet (43.3 m), which is the same as the building's height from top to bottom. It is paved with colored slabs of marble (2). The hemispherical dome ceiling (3) is beautifully decorated with coffers of diminishing size, arranged in five rows. A large circular opening lights up the interior (4), and rain pours through on wet days. On the walls are six side niches (5), an apse (6), and eight shrines. The techniques used to build the Pantheon (particularly the dome) are still discussed today.

Building walls

The earliest construction technique for building walls involved placing dry square stones or volcanic tufo blocks one on top of the other; this method was called *opus quadratum* (1). In the *opus incertum* technique, a kind of concrete was poured into the gap between two stone or brick walls (2). Later, walls were made using the *opus reticulum* method (3), in which small, pyramid-shaped blocks of tufo were laid in a net pattern, and strengthened at the corners with larger blocks of tufo. From the time of Caesar onward, brick walls were built using the most common technique, *opus testaceum* (4).

Altar of Peace

The "Altar of Peace" (*Ara Pacis*) is a splendid example of art from the time of Emperor Augustus. The altar stands on a podium inside a roofless rectangular enclosure, which is decorated on the inside with plant motifs. Around the outside, the Imperial family is shown walking in procession toward the altar. Augustus, his wife Livia, and General Agrippa are all identifiable.

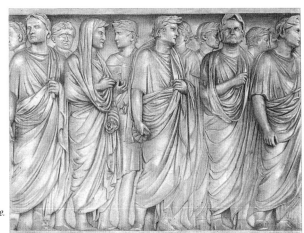

Detail from the Ara Pacis *frieze.*

The Colosseum

The great amphitheater in Rome was begun during the reign of Emperor Vespasian (69–79 CE), and opened by Emperor Titus in 80 CE. It was immediately called the *Colosseum* because of a colossal bronze statue measuring almost 100 feet (30.5 m) high that stood nearby. The colosseum is about 620 feet (189 m) by 512 feet (156 m) at its longest and widest points. The outer wall is 4 stories high, and the bottom three levels contain 80 arches each. Steps up from the ground level gave the public a quick entry and exit to the seating areas, which were arranged in 7 tiers. A canvas awning protected spectators from the sun.

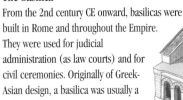

The basilica

From the 2nd century CE onward, basilicas were built in Rome and throughout the Empire. They were used for judicial administration (as law courts) and for civil ceremonies. Originally of Greek-Asian design, a basilica was usually a rectangular hall, sometimes divided by columns, with a semicircular apse, or recess, at one end. The exterior was often surrounded by porticos, where traders sold goods and bankers changed money.

The vast scale of the Massenzio Basilica reflected the grandiose style of late Imperial architecture.

Tomb of Cecilia Metella, on the Appian Way.

Tombs

Roman architects designed many splendid funerary buildings. Some were huge in size, and were built in a special style. This tomb from the early 1st century CE was the tomb of the noblewoman Cecilia Metella. Its foundation of travertine stone blocks is covered by an internal dome, which supports a battlemented tower.

Town-planning

Until the mid-1st century CE, Rome expanded without any strict controls. The construction work that followed the great fire of 64 CE, under Emperor Nero, attempted to restore some order to the chaotic road layout, but because the city was so busy and so highly populated, it was an impossible task. The result was a patchwork of well-planned, spacious areas alongside crowded quarters, where the poor lived in multistory rented apartment blocks (*insulae*).

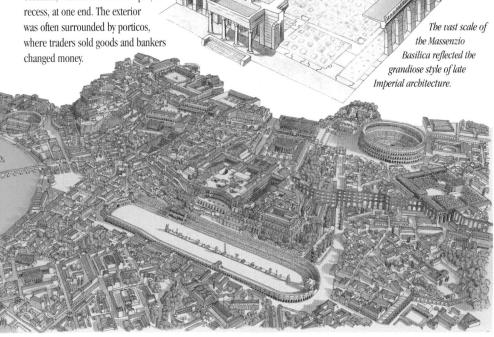

Housing

A constant problem in ancient Rome was the shortage of housing. Wealthy citizens and families of long-standing lived in private dwellings (*domus*) in the more attractive parts of the city. But the majority of the population lived in large apartment blocks (*insulae*) in the poorer districts, where collapsing buildings and fires were a common problem. A census taken in Rome in the 2nd century CE recorded 1,797 *domus* and 40,602 *insulae*. Prosperous families often owned a villa in the country as well as a house in the city.

Due to a lack of building land, housing in Rome developed upward. Apartment blocks were built around an inner courtyard and sometimes reached six stories high. They were divided into rented living quarters. The rooms were damp and almost without light, and they had no fireplace, running water, or sanitation.

Cupboards

The cupboard was a typically Roman piece of furniture, unknown to the Greeks. They were always made of wood and had paneled doors, bone hinges, and metal handles. The shelves inside were used for storing domestic items or provisions.

The upper part of this unusual cupboard from Herculaneum was made to look like a temple, and was used to store statuettes of the Lares, the household gods. The lower part has folding doors that swing back on themselves to give two opening positions.

Numerous terracotta oil-lamps like this one have been found.

Lighting

Roman houses were not well lit. Daylight was the main source of light. At dusk, wax or tallow candles and oil lamps with wicks were lit. Oil lamps were generally made of terracotta or bronze, but following the growing taste for luxury items, some ornamental versions were made from silver or gold. In the grander houses, oil lamps with several burners hung on chains from the ceilings or stood on supporting stands.

An elegant house of the 2nd century BCE

A private house (*domus*) was usually built around a courtyard (*atrium*) (1). In the center of the *atrium* was a basin (2), which collected rainwater through an opening in the roof (3). The dining room (*triclinium*) (4) was next to the garden, and was furnished with couches and small portable tables. In the adjacent kitchen (5), slaves prepared food. One or more of the rooms opening onto the street (6) might be rented to storekeepers. The *domus* was usually a single-story building, but some houses had a second story, which provided space for extra bedrooms (7). From the 2nd century BCE, the *domus* became more spacious. It had a larger garden containing fountains and works of art, surrounded by a covered colonnade (*peristyle*) (8).

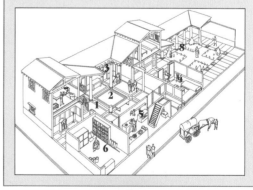

Heating

Rich people's houses were well heated by hot air that circulated in spaces beneath the floors or inside the walls. Braziers of various shapes and sizes provided extra heat, and could be moved from room to room as needed. Sometimes they were even suspended from the ceilings.

A portable bronze brazier decorated with theatrical masks, from Herculaneum. It has a hot water tank inside.

This floor mosaic of a guard dog was found at the entrance of a house in Pompeii. Such pictures were often accompanied by the warning words "Beware of the dog!"

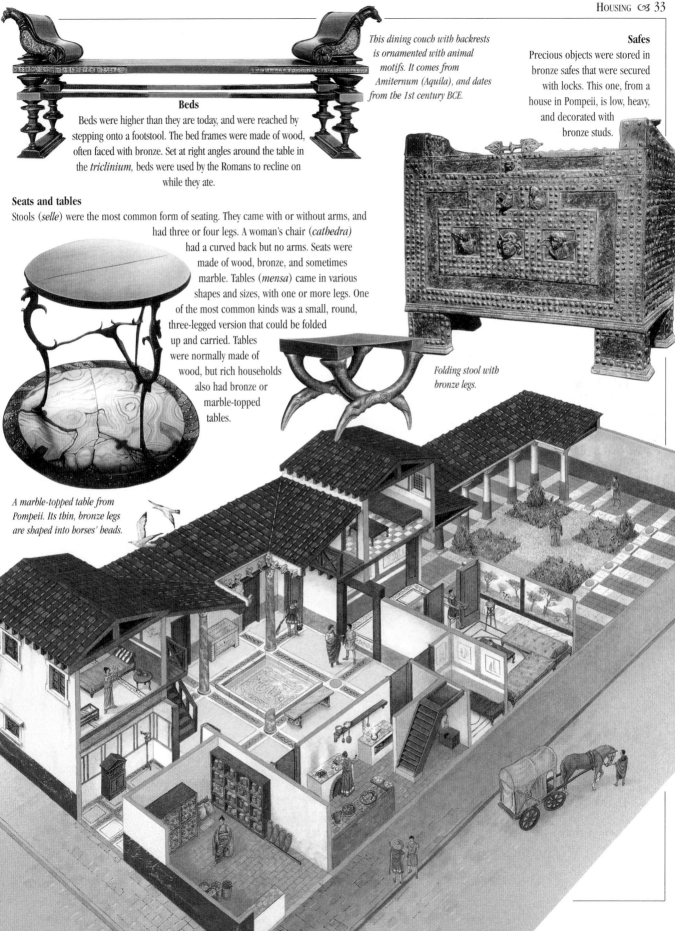

This dining couch with backrests is ornamented with animal motifs. It comes from Amiternum (Aquila), and dates from the 1st century BCE.

Beds

Beds were higher than they are today, and were reached by stepping onto a footstool. The bed frames were made of wood, often faced with bronze. Set at right angles around the table in the *triclinium,* beds were used by the Romans to recline on while they ate.

Seats and tables

Stools (*selle*) were the most common form of seating. They came with or without arms, and had three or four legs. A woman's chair (*cathedra*) had a curved back but no arms. Seats were made of wood, bronze, and sometimes marble. Tables (*mensa*) came in various shapes and sizes, with one or more legs. One of the most common kinds was a small, round, three-legged version that could be folded up and carried. Tables were normally made of wood, but rich households also had bronze or marble-topped tables.

Folding stool with bronze legs.

A marble-topped table from Pompeii. Its thin, bronze legs are shaped into horses' heads.

Safes

Precious objects were stored in bronze safes that were secured with locks. This one, from a house in Pompeii, is low, heavy, and decorated with bronze studs.

New settlements

In far-flung places along the borders of the Empire, towns soon sprang up around Roman military encampments. Local small traders set up stores to supply the legionaries with their daily comforts. When discharged from the army, many Roman soldiers settled in these new towns and married local women. Over time, as borders were extended and the army moved its quarters elsewhere, the original encampment area became the heart of the new city, with grid-pattern roads, city gates, and fortifications.

A relief on Trajan's Column in Rome shows Roman soldiers building the defensive wall of a permanent encampment. In time, the walled area would become the heart of a new city.

The Nigri (black) Gate in Trier, Germany, provided access to the city.

Roman Cities

The Romans founded cities throughout Italy and the Empire. Many new towns sprang up around military encampments, especially on the Empire's borders. When the Romans conquered a city, they quickly erected fine public buildings – temples, amphitheaters, public baths, and colonnaded squares – as a way of imposing the Roman way of life on the local people. Many modern cities are built on the sites of ancient Roman towns, and in some of them the original Roman street plan has survived almost intact.

From military encampment to city

Roman cities (see plan, right) that developed on the sites of former military encampments preserved their square plan and the grid-pattern roads. The roads ran *cardo* (north to south) and *decumanus* (east to west). The areas once used for exercising troops became public squares and market places, and baths, theaters, and amphitheaters were soon built. Linked by roads used by the army, these new towns soon became rich and prosperous commercial centers.

The amphitheater in Verona in northeastern Italy has survived largely intact.

The amphitheater

Amphitheaters were built as venues for entertainment of all kinds, and they were one of the great creations of Roman architecture. Tiered seating for the public surrounded an oval arena, where animal fights, hunts, and gladiator fights were held. Occasionally the arena was flooded so that naval battles could be staged.

Temples

A Roman temple was not just an imposing building; it was also a way of spreading Roman culture. Derived from the Greek model, it stood on a high podium and was reached by a central flight of steps. Corinthian columns surrounded the front.

This temple in Nimes, France, is dedicated to Emperor Augustus's prematurely deceased heirs, Gaius and Lucius Caesar.

The Baths of Caracalla

Built in Rome early in the 2nd century CE by Emperor Caracalla, the baths covered about 1.4 million square feet (130,064 sq m) and could accommodate 1,600 bathers. They were fed by a branch of the Aqua Marcia aqueduct. Romans usually went to the baths in the afternoon. They left their clothes in the dressing room (1), exercised in the gym (2), and had their skin smoothed and oiled in the *unctuaria* (3). They then swam in the *natatio* (4), an open-air swimming pool, or went to the *tepidarium*, a large constantly heated room (5), then to the lofty *calidarium,* with its great dome, for a hot bath (6), and to the adjoining saunas (7). The visit ended with a dive into the cold waters of the *frigidarium* (8).

Water

One of the advantages of living in a city was the abundance of water. Public fountains and baths were continually supplied with water by the aqueducts. Some citizens were allowed to channel off water for their private use.

Public fountain in a street in Pompeii.

Squares

The heart of a city was the main square in the forum. Even when a city expanded, the square remained the center of political, religious, and economic life. Surrounding it were the principal administrative buildings, temples, market, and rooms of the money changers, who also acted as bankers.

The square in the forum of Pompeii was surrounded on three sides by a covered colonnade, and dominated by the Temples of Jove and Apollo.

Trajan's Arch was opened for public use in 114 CE. It marked the start of the new extension of the Appian Way – the main road linking Benevento in south-central Italy with the southern port of Brindisi.

Triumphal arches

Triumphal arches were built on Roman roads throughout the Empire. They were simple in form, and ornamented with elaborate carvings designed to carry a political message. Traditionally, the side facing the city was ornamented with scenes of peace, and the side facing the countryside depicted military encounters.

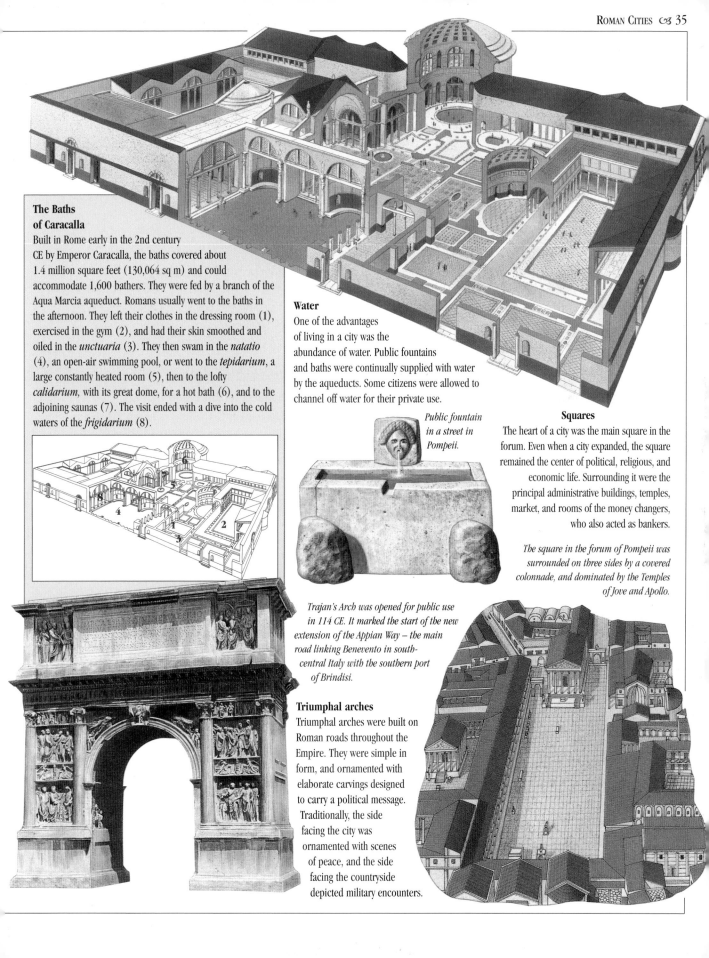

Glossary

amphitheater A Roman structure that housed large spectator events.

barbarian A member of a community not associated with an established civilization; loosely, an outsider.

Carthage An ancient city founded by the Phoenicians, who fought with Rome during the Punic Wars, and destroyed by Romans in 146 BCE.

cavalry A group of soldiers that fights on horseback.

Christianity The religion that follows the teachings of Jesus Christ.

colosseum The official name of the main amphitheater in Rome, which housed 50,000 spectators.

currency A system of money used in a particular civilization or society.

emperor The supreme ruler over an empire.

empire A vast group of territories ruled by one government or ruler.

herbs Plants that are used for medicinal or culinary purposes.

imperial Of or relating to an empire or the exploits associated with the growth of an empire.

medicinal Describing anything that relates to medicine or is used to cure illness or disease.

Mediterranean Relating to the regions or culture of the Mediterranean Sea, which is situated between Europe and Africa.

Mesopotamia A region in southwest Asia, widely regarded as the cradle of civilization.

Nile River A major river in Africa that is regarded as the longest in the world.

Pompeii An ancient city in southern Italy that was destroyed by the eruption of Mount Vesuvius in 79 CE.

republic A government whose citizens have significant voting power.

trident A weapon or hunting tool that is fashioned as a spear with three prongs.

For More Information

American Institute for Roman Culture

U.S. Academic Relations Office

3800 North Lamar Boulevard

Suite 730-174

Austin, TX 78756

(512) 772-1844

Web site: http://www.romanculture.org

The American Institute for Roman Culture is dedicated to both promoting and preserving the culture of the great civiliation of Rome.

Archaeological Institute of America

Boston University

656 Beacon Street

Boston, MA 02215

(617) 353-9361

Web site: http://www.archaeological.org

The Archaeological Institute of America is North America's oldest and largest organization dedicated to the study of the history of the world through archaeology.

British Museum

Ancient Rome

Great Russell Street, WC1B 3DG

London, England

http://www.britishmuseum.org/explore/world_cultures/europe/ancient_rome.aspx

The British Museum is one of the world's most respected museums. It houses numerous exhibitions, including those related to ancient Rome.

Joseph Campbell Foundation

P.O. Box 36

San Anselmo, CA 94979

(800) 330-6987

Web site: http://www.jcf.org

The Joseph Campbell Foundation is a nonprofit organization dedicated to preserving the scholarship of Joseph Campbell, one of the most accomplished scholars of mythology, whose work included the study of ancient Rome.

Kidipede

Ancient Rome – History for Kids

2007 NE 25th Avenue

Portland, OR 97212

Web site: http://www.historyforkids.org/learn/romans

Kidepede is a Web site that offers young people a wealth of information on history.

Web Sites

Due to the changing nature of Internet links, Rosen Publishing has developed an online list of Web sites related to the subject of this book. This site is updated regularly. Please use this link to access the list:

http://www.rosenlinks.com/aac/rome

For Further Reading

Adams, Simon. *Life in Ancient Rome* (Kingfisher Knowledge). New York, NY: Kingfisher, 2005.

Bargallo i Chaves, Eva. *Rome* (Ancient Civilizations). New York, NY: Chelsea House Publications, 2005.

Chrisp, Peter. *Ancient Rome* (History in Art). Chicago, IL: Raintree, 2005.

Crompton, Samuel Willard. *Julius Caesar* (Ancient World Leaders). New York, NY: Chelsea House Publications, 2003.

Forsyth, Fiona. *Augustus: The First Emperor* (Leaders of Ancient Rome). New York, NY: Rosen Publishing Group, 2003.

Lassieur, Allison. *The Ancient Romans* (People of the Ancient World). New York, NY: Children's Press, 2005.

Nardo, Don. *Arts, Leisure and Entertainment: Life of the Ancient Romans*. New York, NY: Lucent Books, 2003.

Nardo, Don. (Editor). *Exploring Cultural History — Living in Ancient Rome*. Farmington Hills, MI: Greenhaven Press, 2003.

Nardo, Don. *Daily Life — Games of Ancient Rome*. Chicago, IL: KidHaven Press, 2005.

Nardo, Don. *From Founding to Fall: A History of Rome*. New York, NY: Lucent Books, 2003.

Nardo, Don. *Words of the Ancient Romans: Primary Sources*. New York, NY: Lucent Books, 2003.

Tracy, Kathleen. *The Life & Times Of Constantine* (Biography from Ancient Civilizations). Hockessin, DE: Mitchell Lane Publishers, 2005.

Index

Adriatic coast 16
Aeneas 26
Aeneid 26, 29
Aesculepius (Asclepius) 26
Africa 6, 16, 17, 20
Agrippa, Marcus, general 30, 31
Albania 9
Alexandria 17
Altar of Peace (*Ara Pacis*) 31
Amiternum (Aquila) 33
Ancona 28
Antinous 29
Antoninus, emperor 11
Apollo 12, 35
Apollonius of Athens 7
Appian way 16, 31, 35
Aqua Marcia, aqueduct 27, 35
Aquileia 14
Arch of Septimius Severus 7
Armenia 10
Ars Medica 26
Asia 12
Asia Minor 20
Assyria 10
Atlantic coast 17
Atlas 26
Augustus, emperor 6, 9, 10, 11, 23, 26,
    31, 34
Aurora 11

Bacchus (Dionysus) 12
Baiae 10
Barbarians 10, 11, 28
Barbegal 27
Basilica Iulia 7
Baths of Caracalla 35
Bay of Naples 21
Benevento 35
Brindisi 16, 35
Britain 6, 9, 18

Caesar, Gaius 34
Caesar, Julius 7, 9, 22, 30
Caesar, Lucius 34
Caligula, emperor 11
Camilli 13
Campania 8
Caracalla, emperor 35
Carthage 17
Carthaginians 6, 19
Cato 20
Ceres (Demeter) 12
Christianity 12, 13, 28
Cicero, Marcus Tullius 26
Colosseum 31
Columella 20
Constantine, emperor 11, 13, 28
Constantius Chlorus, emperor 11

Consuls 8
Crassus, commander 11
Cybele 12
Cyrene 20

Dacia 10, 19
Dacian wars 28
Dante 10
Danube River 19
Diocletian, emperor 11
Domitian, emperor 11

Earth 11
Eastern Roman Empire 11
Egypt 12, 15, 17
Ennius 22
Ephesus 26
Etruria 8
Etruscans 8, 12, 28, 29

Fortuna Primigenia 12
Fortuna Sanctuary 9
Forum 7, 14, 15, 19
France 9, 27, 34

Gades (Cadiz) 17
Galen of Pergamum 26
Galerius, emperor 11
Gaul 9
Germans 19
Germany 11, 34
Greece 12, 16, 26
Greek colonies 12
Greek colonists 20
Greek language 26
Greeks 6, 7, 19, 24, 26, 28, 29, 32

Hadrian, emperor, 10, 28, 29, 30
Hadrian's Wall 18
Helen, saint 28
Heosphorus 11
Heracles 12
Herculaneum 14, 23, 28, 32
Hercules (Heracles) 12, 18, 29
House of the Golden Bracelet 29
Hungary 11

Isis 11
Italic peoples 6, 28

Jerusalem 19
Jesus Christ 13
Jove (Zeus) 12, 35
Juno (Hera) 12
Jupiter 18

Lares 13, 32
Latin 26

Latin people 6
Livia 10, 31
Livius Andronicus 22
Livius's House 28

Manes 13
Marcellus 22
Marcus Aurelius, emperor 11, 26, 28
Mars 13, 18
Massenzio Basilica 31
Maximian, emperor 11
Mediterranean Sea 6, 8
Mercury (Hermes) 12, 14
Mesopotamia 6, 10
Metella, Cecilia 31
Metamorphoses 29
Milazzo 19
Milvian bridge 16
Minerva 12, 24
Mithra 12
Monarchy 6

Naevius 22
Naples 16
Neptune 13, 17
Nero, emperor 11, 13, 31
Nigri Gate 34
Nile River 9, 12
Nimes 34
Nocera 23

Octavian, see Augustus, emperor
Osimo 28
Osiris 12
Ostia 15, 17
Ovid 29

Palatine Hill 8
Palestrina 9, 12
Pannonia 11
Pantheon 30
Parthians 10, 11
Patricians 8
Penates 13
Phraates IV, king of Parthians 11
Plautus 22
Plebeians 8
Pompeii 7, 9, 14, 20, 21, 22, 23, 24, 26,
    28, 29, 32, 33, 35
Pompey 9
Pozzuoli 16
Pyrrhus, king of Epirus 9

Ravenna 11
Remus 8
Republic 6, 8
Roma 6
Roman law 6

Romania 10, 19
Romulus 8
Romulus Augustulus 10

Salus 26
Segovia 27
Senate 6, 8, 9, 11
Servian walls 8
Servius Tullius, king 8
Seville 10
Sicily 16
Slaves 6, 14, 27
Spain 10, 17
Spanish peninsula 6
Stabia 17
State Treasury 7

Tabularium 7
Taranto 9
Temple of Concord 7
Temple of Saturn 7
Temple of Vespasian 7
Terence 22
Tetrarchy 11
Thessaly 10
Tiber River 8, 15, 16, 17
Tiberius, emperor 11
Titus Arch 19
Titus, emperor 31
Tivoli 10, 28
Trajan, emperor 10, 14, 16, 19, 27, 28
Trajan's Arch 35
Trajan's Column 28, 34
Trier 25, 34

Valley of Thebes 10
Varro 20
Venus (Aphrodite) 12
Verona 34
Vespasian, emperor 31
Vesta 13
Vesuvius, volcano 14
Vettii house 29
Via Flaminia 16
Virgil 26, 29
Vittimari 13

Western Roman Empire 11

About the Author

Nicholas Pistone is a writer living in New York.

The publishers would like to thank the following picture libraries and photographers for permission to reproduce their photos:

Cover (right, top to bottom): © www.istockphoto.com/Duncan Walker, © www.istockphoto.com/mddphoto, © www.istockphoto.com/Serdar Yagci, © www.istockphoto.com/Hedda Gjerpen.

9 Scala Group, Florence; 11 Scala Group, Florence; 12–13 Scala Group, Florence; 15 Scala Group, Florence; 17 Scala Group, Florence; 19 Scala Group, Florence; 21 Scala Group, Florence; 22 Scala Group, Florence; 24 Scala Group, Florence; 27 Scala Group, Florence; 29 Scala Group, Florence; 30 Archivi Alinari, Florence.